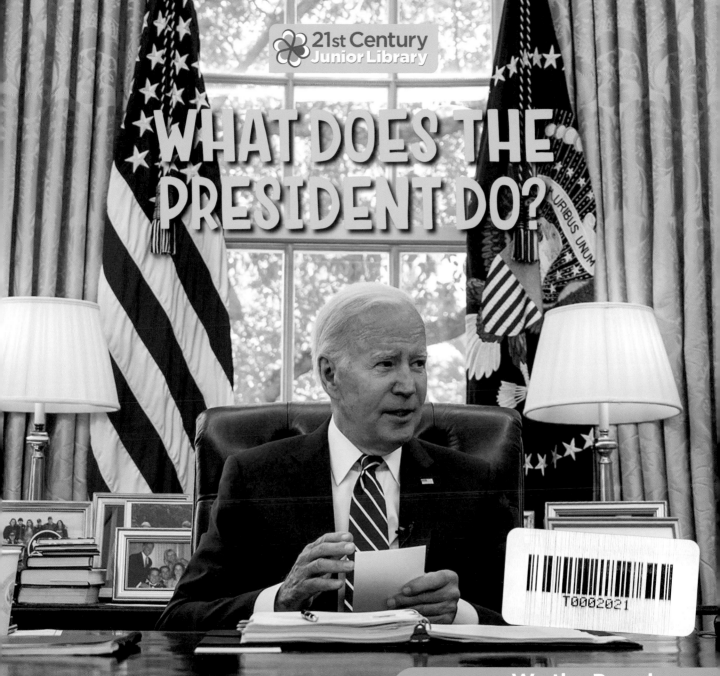

WHAT DOES THE PRESIDENT DO?

21st Century Junior Library

Kevin Winn

We the People:
U.S. Government at Work

Published in the United States of America by:

CHERRY LAKE PRESS

2395 South Huron Parkway, Suite 200, Ann Arbor, Michigan 48104
www.cherrylakepress.com

Reading Adviser: Beth Walker Gambro, MS, Ed., Reading Consultant, Yorkville, IL
Content Adviser: Mark Richards, Ph.D., Professor, Dept. of Political Science, Grand Valley State University, Allendale, MI

Photo Credits: cover: The White House/Flickr; page 5: National Portrait Gallery, Smithsonian Institution; page 6: Architect of the Capitol; page 7: FDR Library; page 8: © Abigail McCann/Shutterstock; page 9: © Aaron of L.A. Photography/Shutterstock (top), The White House (bottom); page 11: Pete Souza/The White House; pages 12, 13: © mark reinstein/Shutterstock; page 14: Photo by Eric Draper, Courtesy of the George W. Bush Presidential Library; page 16 © vesperstock/Shutterstock; page 18: © Made360/Shutterstock; page 19: © Sheila Fitzgerald/Shutterstock; page 20: © wavebreakmedia/Shutterstock; page 21: © Air Images/Shutterstock

Cherry Lake Press is an imprint of Cherry Lake Publishing Group.

Library of Congress Cataloging-in-Publication Data

Names: Winn, Kevin P., author.
Title: What does the president do? / Kevin Winn.
Description: Ann Arbor, Michigan : Cherry Lake Publishing, [2023] | Series: We the people: U.S. government at work | Audience: Grades 2-3
Summary: "Young readers will discover what the U.S. president does and learn about the basic building blocks of U.S. democracy. They'll also learn how they play a key role in American democracy. Series is aligned to 21st Century Skills curriculum standards. Engaging inquiry-based sidebars encourage students to Think, Create, Guess, and Ask Questions. Includes table of contents, glossary, index, author biography, and sidebars"—Provided by publisher.
Identifiers: LCCN 2022039948 | ISBN 9781668919385 (hardcover) | ISBN 9781668920404 (paperback) | ISBN 9781668921739 (ebook) | ISBN 9781668923061 (pdf)
Subjects: LCSH: Presidents—United States—Juvenile literature. | Executive power—United States—Juvenile literature. | United States—Politics and government—Juvenile literature.
Classification: LCC JK517 .W57 2023 | DDC 352.230973—dc23/eng/20220923
LC record available at https://lccn.loc.gov/2022039948

Cherry Lake Press would like to acknowledge the work of the Partnership for 21st Century Learning, a Network of Battelle for Kids. Please visit http://www.battelleforkids.org/networks/p21 for more information.

Printed in the United States of America
Corporate Graphics

CONTENTS

THE HISTORY OF THE U.S. PRESIDENT

The president of the United States is the leader of the U.S. government. It's a powerful job. This power helps the president lead the country. The president represents the United States.

When the United States became a country, it needed a leader. The founders didn't want a king. They had a king when they were part of Great Britain. They fought to become their own country.

George Washington was the first president of the United States.

They wanted to avoid another **monarchy**. They saw the importance of having a leader with limited power. This made the United States different from other countries in the world.

People from **diverse** backgrounds can run for president, but there are some rules. First, a person must be at least 35 years old. Second, they must be a **natural-born citizen**.

The United States Constitution was signed in 1787.

Franklin D. Roosevelt is the only U.S. president to serve more than two terms. He was elected four times. The Constitution was then amended to only allow a person to serve two terms as president. What are the advantages of this? What are the disadvantages?

Finally, they must have lived continuously in the United States for at least 14 years.

Presidents are **elected**. They serve for a term of 4 years and can be elected twice. This is because the Twenty-second **Amendment** to the **Constitution** placed a term limit on the presidency. Before 1951, presidents could serve for unlimited terms.

When someone **campaigns** for president, they choose a running mate. If elected, the running mate becomes vice president. The vice president holds a very powerful position. The vice president is first in line to become president if the president should die or not be able to serve. As of 2022, all presidents have been men, but women have run as well.

Kamala Harris is the first woman to be vice president.

THE PRESIDENT'S DUTIES

Once elected, what can the president do? One **responsibility** is making sure laws are followed. After Congress approves a **bill**, the president can decide to either **veto** or sign it. If the president signs it, the bill becomes a law.

Once a bill arrives at the president's desk, the president has 10 days to veto or sign it.

The U.S. president is also the leader of the military. This is why the president is also called the commander in chief. While Congress holds the power to declare war, the military follows the president's orders to carry out missions.

The president also represents the United States. Presidents work with leaders from other countries. They **negotiate** and sign **treaties**. For instance, leaders of countries signed the Treaty of Versailles in 1919. This treaty officially ended World War I.

President Bill Clinton (right) meets with Russian president Boris Yeltsin in 1994.

President George W. Bush gives a State of the Union Address to Congress.

Create!

The president serves you. What's an issue you care about? Write a letter to the president explaining the issue and why they should care about it too. Mail your letter to:

The White House
1600 Pennsylvania Avenue, N.W.
Washington, DC 20500

Treaties can be about many things, like ending wars, trading goods and services, and ensuring **human rights**. These are the freedoms that should belong to all people.

Each year, the president updates everyone about how the country is doing. This is called the State of the Union Address. The president gives this speech using radio, television, and the internet to reach as many people as possible.

Look!

How do the people around you get involved in presidential elections? Do they place signs in their yards or windows? Do you see t-shirts supporting a candidate? Think about ways you can get involved in presidential elections. Even though you're not old enough to vote, you still have a voice!

HOLDING THE PRESIDENT RESPONSIBLE

Staying **informed** about what the president does is important. It helps you decide if they are doing their job well. Understanding the president's words and actions helps us decide if they should keep their job.

While the president has a lot of power, so do we—the people. We vote and elect our leader. The presidency is a powerful position, but we hold the power to decide who becomes president.

Ask Questions!

Many people choose not to vote. Why do you think this is? What stops people from voting? How can you encourage others to vote?

VOTING IS MY SUPER POWER

ACTIVITY

Get creative! Pick someone you think would make a great president. Why do you think they'll make a great leader? Discuss your reasons with a friend or family member. Then make a campaign sign for them!

GLOSSARY

amendment (uh-MEND-muhnt) change or addition to the U.S. Constitution

bill (BIL) draft of a law

campaigns (kam-PAYNS) runs for an office

constitution (kahn-stuh-TOO-shuhn) set of rules that guides a country

diverse (dih-VUHRSS) having different qualities or backgrounds

elected (uh-LEK-tuhd) voted into a position

human rights (HYOO-muhn RYTES) powers and freedoms that all people should have

informed (in-FORMD) have knowledge of

monarchy (MAH-nuhr-kee) government led by a king or queen

natural-born citizen (NAH-chuh-ruhl SIH-tuh-zuhn) someone born within the United States, its territories, or districts

negotiates (nih-GOH-shee-aytz) discusses with others in order to form an agreement

responsibility (rih-spawn-suh-BIH-luh-tee) duty or something a person must do

treaties (TREE-teez) agreements with another country

veto (VEE-toh) strike down or go against

FIND OUT MORE

Books

Baxter, Roberta. *The Creation of the U.S. Constitution.* Ann Arbor, MI: Cherry Lake Publishing, 2014.

Bedesky, Baron. *What is a Government?* New York, NY: Crabtree Publishing Co., 2008.

Cheney, Lynne. *We the People.* New York, NY: Simon & Schuster, 2012.

Christelow, Eileen. *Vote!* New York, NY: Clarion Books, 2018.

Orr, Tamra. *Barack Obama's Inaugural Address.* Ann Arbor, MI: Cherry Lake Publishing, 2020.

Websites

Ben's Guide to the U.S. Government
https://bensguide.gpo.gov
Let Ben Franklin guide you through the whos and whats of our government.

iCivics
https://icivics.org
Find out how you can be an informed and involved citizen.

INDEX

ABOUT THE AUTHOR

Kevin Winn is a children's book writer and researcher. He focuses on issues of racial justice and educational equity in his work. In 2020, Kevin earned his doctorate in Educational Policy and Evaluation from Arizona State University.